Cracker Barrel
Recipes

Unlock the Secrets for the Best Copycat Cracker Barrel Dishes to Make Favorite Menu Items at Home. From Breakfast to Dessert to Satisfy your Southern Food Craving

Kaylee Hooper

Table of Contents

Introduction

Cracker Barrel History and Facts

Cracker Barrel was set up in 1969 by Dan Evinsand, a sales agent for Shell Oil, who produced the restaurant and gift shop notion initially to enhance gas sales. Made to resemble the conventional state shop he recalled from his youth, using a title picked to provide it with a Southern state motif, Cracker Barrel was initially meant to pull the attention of airport travelers. The first restaurant was constructed near Interstate 40 in Lebanon, Tennessee. It started in September 1969, serving Southern cuisines such as snacks, grits, country ham, and turnip greens.

Evins integrated Cracker Barrel in February 1970 and opened more places. From early 1970s, the company leased property on gas station websites around interstate highways to construct restaurants. These ancient places all featured petrol pumps onsite; throughout gas shortages in the middle of the late 1970s, the Company started to create restaurants with no pumps. In early 1980s, the business reduced the number of gasoline stations onsite, finally phasing them out entirely since the firm focused on its restaurant and current sales earnings.

Cracker Barrel turned into a publicly traded firm in 1981 to increase funds for additional growth. It floated over half of a million shares, raising $4.6 million. After the first public offering, Cracker Barrel climbed at a speed of approximately 20% annually; from 1987, the firm had turned into a series of over 50 units in 8 countries, with annual net earnings of nearly $81 million.

New niches and refocus

The organization climbed continuously during the 1980s and 1990s, reaching a 1 billion dollar market worth by 1992. In 1993, the profits of the series were almost double that of any other restaurant. In 1994, the series analyzed a carry-out-only shop, Cracker Barrel Old Country Store Corner Marketplace, in suburban housing areas.

Additionally, it expanded into new markets throughout the institution of more conventional Cracker Barrel places, nearly all out the South, and analyzed alterations to its own menus to accommodate new areas. The series of different regional dishes into its menus, such as eggs and dinner in Texas and Reuben sandwiches in New York, continued to provide its menu items in most restaurants.

From September 1997, Cracker Barrel's 314 restaurants also aimed to boost the number of shops by roughly 50 each year within the subsequent 5 decades. The company closed its Corner Marketplace surgery in 1997 and refocused its restaurant and gift store places. The organization's president, Ron Magruder, said the series focused on strengthening its core motif, offering conventional retail and food at a state shop atmosphere with excellent service and country songs.

The series opened its first restaurant and gift shop near the road in 1998, in Dothan, Alabama. By 2000s, in the wake of incidents between degrees of racial controversy and discrimination within its policy of shooting gay employees, the business had established a selection of promotional actions such as a nationwide book inducing and sweepstakes with trips to the Country Music Association Awards and rocking chairs among those awards.

Operations

The number of joint restaurants and shops possessed by Cracker Barrel grew between 1997 and 2000, to over 420 places. In 2000 and 2001, the business dealt with staffing and infrastructure problems associated with the accelerated expansion by using a broader recruitment approach and introducing new technologies, such as an order-placement program.

In the late 1990s into the mid-2000s, the Business focused on launching new places in residential areas to draw residents and employees as clients. It upgraded its advertising in 2006 to promote new clients, altering its highway billboard ads to add pictures of menu objects. Formerly the indications had featured just the organization's emblem. From 2011, Cracker Barrel started over 600 restaurants in 42 nations. On January 17, 2012, firm founder Dan Evins died of bladder cancer.

Food and present store

Cracker Barrel serves traditional Southern comfort food as a Southern-themed series, frequently referred to as "down- home" nation cooking, and sells gift items such as easy toy agents of the 1950s and 1960s, toy cars puzzles, and woodcrafts. Additionally, sold are country songs, CDs, DVDs of traditional historical TV, Banners, baking mixes, and kitchen novelty decoration, and ancient, timeless brands of sweets and snack meals.

Breakfast is served each day, and you'll discover two choices: just for breakfast, another for lunch and dinner. Due to the fact that the restaurant's open menu comprises showcased Southern specialties like bites, grilled chicken, shellfish, and seasonal menu items added through 1980s and 1990s. In 2007, Cracker Barrel announced plans to expel artificial trans fats from their menu products.

Places, support, and decoration

For much of its ancient history, Cracker Barrel decided to find its restaurants across the Interstate Highway System. The vast majority of its restaurants stay near interstate and other highways. Cracker Barrel is famous for its clients' loyalty, mostly travelers that are very likely to spend more in restaurants than sailors.

The places are all themed around the notion of a conventional Southern U.S. overall shop. Things used to decorate every shop are real artifacts, such as regular items in the early 1900s and afterward.

Each area comes with an outdoor porch lined with hardwood rocking chairs, a wooden peg solitaire game to each dining table, and a rock fireplace with bullhead exhibited over the mantel. In reality, every place has 5 ordinary things: a shotgun, a cookstove, a deer head, a phone, and a traffic light.

Peg games are found in Cracker Barrel because the launch of this very first shop also continues to be made in precisely the same household in Lebanon, Tennessee. The decorations at every location typically contain artifacts linked to the history of the region, such as classic household tools, older wall calendars, and advertisement posters, and classic photos; those are centrally kept in a warehouse in Tennessee, where they're cataloged and stockpiled for future usage by individual shop locations.

Prizes

Destination's magazine has introduced the series awards for the best chain restaurant, also in 2010 and 2011, and the Zagat survey called it the "Best Breakfast." The Outdoor Advertising Association of America has chosen the series since the 2011 OBIE Hall of Fame Award recipient for its longstanding utilization of outdoor advertising. It was also called the "Best Family Dining" Restaurant, with a nationally "Choice in Chains" consumer survey in Restaurants & Institutions magazine for 19 consecutive years.

Board of Managers

The organization is conducted by a board of supervisors composed of mostly company outsiders, as is customary for publicly traded firms. Board members are elected each year to the yearly shareholders' assembly, working with a vast majority voting method. There are five committees within the board that manage particular things.

About July 10, 2020, Cracker Barrel Old Country Store noted that successful immediately, Gilbert Dávila was appointed to the provider's supervisors' board. Mr. Dávila is currently the creator and CEO of DMI Consulting, a significant foreign communication, diversity & improvement, and innovation business in the USA, mostly helping fortune 200 companies to construct aggressive development plans predicated on America's fastest-growing population/section.

Investment and Company model

Cracker Barrel restaurants have been targeted toward the household and casual dining marketplace in addition to retail sales. The series also welcomes individuals traveling to interstate highways, so since the vast majority of its areas are near highway exits. The business has encouraged its price controls.

The business has said its objective would be to maintain employee turnover and provide better-educated employees. Since 1980s, the Company has provided an official training plan with rewards for progressing to its workers.

Community participation

Cracker Barrel has encouraged a vast assortment of charities through one-off contributions, promotional events, and partnerships with charitable organizations. The series has affirmed charities and causes in communities where their restaurants are situated, such as the Gulf Coast following Hurricane Katrina in 2005 and Nashville after intense flooding in 2010.

In the same season, Cracker Barrel established "Cracker Barrel Cares Inc.", an employee-funded non-profit firm that provides help to their workers. In addition, Cracker Barrel has partnered with the Wounded Warrior Project, a charity that helps injured warriors.

In an effort to reconstruct its image after many race-related controversies, the company has supplied a scholarship during the National Black Association (MBA), job skills programs and sponsorships with 100 Black Men of America, and the Restaurant and Lodging Association.

From 1999 to 2001, Cracker Barrel sponsored the NASCAR Atlanta 500 at Atlanta Motor Speedway, as well as the Grand Ole Opry from 2004 through 2009. The Company was the Grand Ole Opry's very first presenting sponsor.

This property allowed the enterprise to produce connections inside the Nashville music business; after that, it entered into a partnership with numerous country music celebrities. The series has created partnerships with Alison Krauss, Charlie Daniels, Josh Turner, Kenny Rogers, Dolly Parton, Alan Jackson, and Alabama to provide CD releases and products.

In 1997, the business bought the Mitchell House in Lebanon, Tennessee. The home was the basic dormitory and faculty for Castle Heights Military Academy that Dan Evins and his son attended. The college closed in 1986 along with construction that had sat vacant since then. Cracker Barrel spent 2000$ to revive the house and used it as a company headquarters from 1999 to 2013.

Conflict with Biglari Holdings

Cracker Barrel's board of directors has been at odds with its most significant shareholder, Biglari Holdings Inc. The proprietor of Biglari Holdings, Sardar Biglari, controls a 19.9% share of the Business, only short of the 20% required to activate a shareholder rights plan, much more often termed a "Poison Pill." The Poison Pill has been followed by Biglari Holdings searched for approval to buy a 49.99% share of the organization and combine the supervisors' board.

Biglari Holdings bought shares of Cracker Barrel in 2011. It has frequently been critical of its transparency to investors, overspending on advertisements, absence of consumer worth and capital funds mismanagement, rather than maximizing customer value. Biglari has asked to be on the board of supervisor's times and continues to be denied each time by a vote of shareholders. Biglari Holdings has also put forward a petition to get a onetime $20/share dividend to tackle perceived excessively conservative capitalization rejected by investors. Cracker Barrel has reacted by asserting Biglari includes a "hidden agenda" and a conflict of interest by holding stocks in different restaurant chains like Steak'n Shake.

Benefits of Copycat Recipes

Kraft Foods vs. Cracker Barrel

In November 2012, Cracker Barrel accredited its title to Smithfield Foods' John Morrell Division in a deal to create a lineup of beef products to be marketed in supermarkets and through other retail stations. In reaction, Kraft Foods registered trademark-infringement litigation in February 2013. Kraft has been offering cheese in retail shops beneath their Cracker Barrel manufacturer since 1954.

The company stated that Cracker Barrel shops hadn't made considerable revenue by retail food items outside of their restaurant shop, and also requested that the Smithfield Foods bargain be nullified from the U.S. District Court in the Northern District of Illinois.

About November 14, 2013, in a unanimous ruling written by Judge Richard Posner, the Seventh Circuit Court of Appeals upheld a ruling by a lower District Court judge awarding an injunction against the sale of all Cracker Barrel meat goods to be marketed at shops. The Seventh Circuit upheld the injunction based on the common similarity of these parties' marks, products, and stations of commerce: "It isn't the simple fact that the parties' commerce is so similar that's crucial, nor the simple fact that the goods are comparable (low-priced packed food items).

It's those similarities combined with the reality that, when Cracker Barrel prevails in this lawsuit, similar goods together with confusingly similar trade titles will be marketed through precisely the same distribution station; grocery shops, and frequently the same supermarket.

In Judge Posner's estimation, all these similarities, regardless of the gaps between the parties' various logos and no matter where the goods are regarding one another in grocery shops, may lead buyers to think each of the Kraft goods bearing the "Cracker Barrel" title was created in affiliation with the Defendant. In economics, this behavior is known as "traditional ahead confusion".

The court further reasoned that the probability of confusion had been exacerbated by the reality that the goods at issue were cheap; consequently, consumers could not inspect their labels.

In reaction to this judgment, Kraft Foods and Cracker Barrel created an arrangement concerning the use of this Cracker Barrel title. In trading for Kraft's falling trademark-infringement suit, Cracker Barrel agreed to market its goods under the new "C.B. Old Country Store."

A Nutrient-Dense Plate

If ready food stems from outside the house, you usually have a limited understanding of the sugar, salt, and oils that are processed. For a simple fact, we additionally employ more into our meal if it's served on the table. You may say just how much sugar, salt, and petroleum have been used because you prepare foods in your home

Improved Fruit and Vegetable Intake

By providing you with the ease of cooking in your home, you've got total control over the food that you eat. The thing to note is that your focus will continue together with the ingestion of fruit and vegetables. Attach them to your cooking, bite them or swap them together with your relatives in their way. Take action towards organic choices. Additionally, it's almost always far better to eat whole vegetables and fruits, whether organic, compared to processed foods.

Save Cash and Use What You've Got

Simply because you have not seen your regional health food or meal shop this week does not mean that you have become stuck carrying on. Open your cabinet and refrigerator and determine what may result in a meal. It is often as simple as gluten-free pasta, roasted tomatoes, carrots, frozen veggies, and lemon juice. This very simple meal is stuffed with protein, fiber, vitamins, and nutritional supplements. On top of that, in under 30 minutes, it's flavorful and can be ready. It saves you cash in the future and allows you adequate food to talk about or to get rest the following day.

Sensible Snacking

Bringing premade snacks conserves time, but what goes back to what is in those products? You do not need to give your favorite snacks, but there's a means to make them fitter and frequently taste better. Alter your chips and then dip the chopped veggies into the hummus. Make your snacks with margarine potato chips or carrots. Have a bowl and produce your popcorn in addition to your stove or at the popcorn system. It's possible to control the quantity of sugar, salt, and petroleum included.

Share Your Delicious Health

As soon as you create your meals, you're so pleased with your accomplishments. What's more, the food tastes great. Don't get me confused today, a few of your creative recipes will not taste exactly the same thing. However, your cuisine is going to be loved by family and friends with continuous experimentation and practice. You may see them enjoy the very greatest nutritious food for you and your beliefs in distributing love and health.

This will provide you with an opportunity to reconnect

Cooking together could provide you with an opportunity to reconnect with your spouse and your nearest and dearest. Cooking also offers other added benefits. The American Psychological Association claims that working with new items, such as learning about a new recipe, will help preserve the connection between a set.

It is Demonstrated to be fitter

You've got total control over what's in your meals if you set up new products jointly or send them directly to your door working with a firm like Plated. This can create a difference in your general wellbeing.

It is a time saver

Components of purchasing would be to await food travel or come to receive it. It might take a lot longer, exactly what time you purchase, and whether the shipping person is great at the instructions! It does not need to take time to cook at home when you do not desire it. You eliminate the requirement to hunt for ingredients or foodstuffs using a service such as Plated. Whatever you will need is on your property, at the specific quantity that you use.

It may be a money saver, also

In the very long term, home-cooked food can help save you money. An assortment of basic ingredients comes at a lower cost than a dish. You can even eat more of a meal at home than if you purchase takeout or take a break to operate the following moment. After a few weeks, you'll notice huge savings beginning to accumulate.

It is personalized

Cooking in your home provides you the opportunity to relish the food that you need, the way you enjoy it. For starters, use Plated if you'd like your meat well-done or fewer candy, the formulation includes suggested adjustments.

Cutting Prices

Everybody probably remembers that it is expensive to eat outside. The disparity between a neighborhood restaurant sandwich along with a kitchen sandwich is much more than a sense. Buying packed food at a restaurant generally costs a lot more than purchasing your merchandise. Cooking in your home will help to get more for your money by increasing the surplus expenses of servicing and cooking restaurants. The more frequently you make your meals, the more cash you save.

Appreciating the Procedure

As soon as you return home on a hectic day, it's a bit more fun than disconnecting from job mails, voicemails, bare missions, or assignments. Cooking at home presents you with a break from your lifestyle and space for creativity. As opposed to hearing noisy messages, then you need to wear the radio, gather spices, and also reflect on the scents that sizzle on the cooker or roast veggies. You could be amazed by just how much you really like once you create a daily custom of preparing meals.

Chapter 1: Breakfast Recipes

1. Ham and Egg Casserole

 Preparation: 5 hours

 Cooking: 20 minutes

 Servings: 2

Ingredients:

- 1/3 C. Lean cooked diced ham (country cured ham if available).
- 1 slice sourdough bread (remove the crust and cut to fit the bottom of the casserole dish).
- 5 beaten eggs. (1 cup)
- 1/4 C. evaporated milk.
- 1/4 tsp. Salt.
- 1/4 tsp. Ground black pepper.
- 1/2 C. Shredded mild cheddar cheese.

Instructions:

1. Preheat the oven to 350 degrees Fahrenheit.
2. Spray a casserole dish with non-stick cooking spray and layer sourdough bread on the bottom.
3. Beat the eggs, season with salt and pepper, then evaporate the milk and carefully combine.
4. Drizzle the egg mixture over the bread.
5. Add the diced ham and shredded cheese over the egg mixture and cover it.
6. Place the casserole in the refrigerator for about 5 hours.
7. Bake for 20 to 22 min., depending on the measurement of the casserole dish.
8. When you shake the container slightly and the eggs do not move, it will be ready.

Nutrition: Calories: 450. Protein: 35 g. Carbs: 21 g. Fat: 25g.

2. Blueberry Syrup

 Preparation: 5 minutes

 Cooking: 15 minutes

 Servings: 3

Ingredients:

- 2 C. Blueberries.
- 1/2 C. Sugar.
- 1 C. water.
- 1 tbsp. Cornstarch.

Instructions:

1. Mix the cornstarch with 2 tbsp. water in a little bowl.
2. Beat until there are no more lumps and set aside.
3. Put the water, blueberries, and sugar into a saucepan.
4. Bring the mixture to a boil, low heat and simmer for about 10 min. until it is reduced a bit.
5. Add in the cornstarch and beat until it is well mixed.
6. Continue to simmer and mix until the sauce has thickened.
7. Once it's gotten to a syrup-like consistency, then remove from the heat.
8. You'll be able to combine using an immersion blender of your choice.
9. Store in the refrigerator for several weeks or in the freezer for several months.
10. Serve cold or hot as you prefer.

Nutrition: Calories: 76. Carbs: 19 g. Sodium 2mg. Sugar 16g.

3. Buttermilk Pancakes

Preparation: 10 minutes

Cooking: 15 minutes

Servings: 4

Ingredients:

- 2 C. all-purpose flour.
- 2 tsp. Baking soda.
- 1 tsp. Salt.
- 1 tbsp. Sugar.
- 2 eggs.
- 2 C. buttermilk.
- Butter for cooking.
- Butter and maple syrup for serving

Instructions:

1. Add all the ingredients to a bowl and mix thoroughly, but don't overdo it.
2. The griddle or nonstick pan should be heated to medium-high heat, and a small amount of butter should be used to oil the pan (more if you like a crispy edge).
3. Using a 1/4-cup measuring cup, drop batter onto the heated pan. Switch and brown the other side once the bottom side is golden.
4. Toss with butter and maple syrup before serving.

Nutrition: Calories: 740. Protein: 9 g. Carbs: 112 g. Fat: 29 g.

4. Loaded Hash Brown Casserole

Preparation: 15 minutes

Cooking: 45 minutes

Servings: 8

Ingredients:

- 1 lb. sausage
- ½ C. American cheese (shredded)
- ½ C. Cheddar cheese (shredded sharp)
- 3 Tbsp. red bell pepper (chopped)
- 2 lb. frozen hashbrowns (thawed)
- 1 1/2 C. shredded Colby cheese (1 C. is for the casserole topping)
- ½ C. Monterey Jack Cheese (shredded)
- 2 Tbsp. butter
- 2 Tbsp. flour
- 2 C. milk

Instructions:

1. Set the oven temperature to 350 °F and preheat it.
2. Reserve 1 cup of Colby cheese for the topping.
3. Brown the sausage in a large skillet over medium heat, breaking it up into little bite-sized pieces as it browns.
4. Add 2 to 3 tbsp of shredded red bell pepper to the sausage when it is almost ready.
5. When the sausage is done cooking, drain it.

6. In a medium-sized saucepan over medium heat, melt 2 tbsp of butter.

7. When the butter has melted, put in 2 tablespoons of flour. Allow the butter and flour to fry for about 1 minute over moderate heat. The flour and butter combination must be cooked together so that the flour does not taste uncooked.

8. Put in 1/4 of the milk until the roux is thickened.

9. When the sauce has thickened, add another 1/4 cup of milk and stir until thickened.

10. Put the excess milk into the sauce. Cook, stirring constantly, until the sauce has thickened.

11. Put in the cheese until it is completely melted.

12. In a large mixing dish, combine hash browns, cheese sauce, and sausage. To blend, put everything together.

13. Transfer the mixture to a 13 x 9-inch baking dish.

14. Garnish with the remaining cup of shredded Colby cheese.

15. Bake for 45 minutes in the oven.

Nutrition: Calories: 515. Protein: 26 g. Carbs: 23 g. Fat: 37g.

5. Hash Brown Casserole

Preparation: 5 minutes

Cooking: 45 minutes

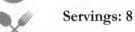

Servings: 8

Ingredients:

- 32 oz. frozen shredded hash browns (defrosted)
- 2 C. colby cheese (grated)
- 1 (10 ¼ oz.) can of chicken soup (cream)
- ½ C. butter (melted)
- 1 pint sour cream
- ½ C. onion (finely chopped)
- ¼ tsp. pepper

Instructions:

1. Heat the oven to 350 °F.
2. Combine all of the ingredients in a large mixing bowl, except for 1/2 cup of the cheese for the topping.
3. Place in a 9x13 casserole dish and top with reserved cheese.
4. Bake for 45–55 minutes, or when the mixture is heated and fluffy.

Nutrition: Calories: 350. Protein: 11 g. Carbs: 26 g. Fat: 26 g.

6. French Toast

Preparation: 10 minutes

Cooking: 25 minutes

Servings: 8

Ingredients:

- 8 slices Texas toast or sourdough bread.
- 4 eggs.
- 1 C. milk.
- 2 tbsp. sugar.
- 4 tsp. vanilla extract.
- 2 pinches salt.

Instructions:

1. Whisk the eggs, sugar, milk, vanilla, and salt in a huge bowl.
2. Heat a griddle or skillet over moderate heat.
3. Spray nonstick cooking spray.
4. Dip each piece of bread into the egg mixture, allowing it to simmer for 25-30 seconds on each side.
5. Move the pieces to a griddle or skillet and cook for 4-5 minutes or until golden brown.
6. Serve with butter and your favorite syrup.

Nutrition: Calories: 460. Protein: 25 g. Carbs: 88 g. Fat: 45 g.

7. Corn Muffin

Preparation: 10 minutes

Cooking: 30 minutes

Servings: 8

Ingredients:

- 3/4 C. yellow cornmeal.
- 1 1/4 C. self-rising flour.
- 1/2 C. Sugar.
- 2 large eggs.
- 2 tbsp. Honey.
- 3/4 C. Buttermilk.
- 1/2 C. unsalted butter (melted and cooled)

Instructions:

1. Preheat the oven to 350°F. Grease a 12-cup muffin pan or line it with paper.
2. Mix the cornmeal, flour, and sugar in a big bowl until well mixed.
3. In a different bowl, whisk the eggs until beaten, then add the honey and buttermilk until completely incorporated.
4. Stirring slowly, add the buttermilk mixture and dissolved butter to the flour. Mix until just blended (there will be lumps). Don't over mix.
5. Pour the batter into the muffin pan, filling each 3/4ths full.
6. Bake in the oven at 350°F for 18-20 min or until muffins are set and tops are lightly browned.
7. Remove from the oven and allow to cool in the pan for 2-3 minutes, then serve hot or let cool on a wire rack.

Nutrition: Calories: 144. Protein: 2 g. Carbs: 20 g. Fat: 6 g.

8. Egg in a Basket

Preparation: 3 minutes

Cooking: 5 minutes

Servings: 1

. . . .

Ingredients:

- 1 slice sourdough bread.
- 1 tbsp. Margarine or butter.
- 1 egg.
- Salt and pepper.

. . . .

Instructions:

1. In a nonstick pan, heat the oil over moderate heat.
2. Indent the sourdough bread slice with a small biscuit cutter or juice jar. Cut a circle in the center of the bread by twisting it slightly. Take out the cut-out circle.
3. Spread margarine or butter on both sides of the bread before placing it in the pan.
4. Put an egg into the hole of the toast.
5. When the bread is toasted on the bottom (approximately 1 minute), switch it over and toast on the other side.
6. To taste, add salt and pepper.

. . . .

Nutrition: Calories: 348. Carbs: 36 g. Protein: 13 g. Fat: 16 g. Sodium: 490 mg

Chapter 2: Lunch Recipes

1. Chicken Casserole

 Preparation: 10 minutes

 Cooking: 60 minutes

 Servings: 4

Ingredients:

Cornbread Topping:

- 1 C. Yellow cornmeal.
- 1/3 C. Flour.
- 1 1/2 tsp. baking powder.
- 1 Tbsp. Sugar.
- 1/2 tsp. Salt.
- 1/2 tsp. Baking soda.
- 2 Tbsp. Vegetable oil.
- 3/4 C. Buttermilk.
- 1 egg.
- ½ C. melted butter

Chicken Casserole Filling:

- 2 1/2 C. chopped cooked chicken breasts.
- 1/4 C. chopped yellow onion
- 1/2 C. sliced celery.
- 1 tsp. Salt.
- 1/4 tsp. freshly ground black pepper.
- 1 can (10, 75 oz.) cream of chicken soup.
- 1 3/4 C. chicken broth.
- 2 Tbsp. Butter.

Instructions:

1. Preheat the oven to 375°F.
2. In a bowl, combine all the cornbread ingredients (except melted butter) until smooth.
3. Pour this mixture into a buttered or greased 8×8-inch dish. Bake for approximately 20-25 min., then remove from oven and let it cool.
4. Crumble cooled cornbread and place 3 C. of cornbread crumbs in a mixing bowl.
5. Add 1/2 C. melted butter to crumbs and mix well, set aside.
6. Create the chicken filling by adding the butter, sauteed onion and celery to a large saucepan on a moderate heat. Cook until tender.
7. Add the chicken broth, cream of chicken soup, salt, and pepper.

8. Stir until all is well mixed.

9. Add the chicken, stir and combine until the mixture reaches a low simmer. Cook for 5 min.

10. Place chicken mixture in 2 1/2 quart buttered the casserole dish or individual casserole dishes (about 4).

11. Topping with the cornbread mixture and transferring into the preheated oven at 350°F.

12. Bake for 35-40 minutes for 35-40 minutes.

Nutrition: Calories: 579. Total Fat: 27 g. Carbs: 48 g, Protein: 38 g.

2. Sunday Chicken

Preparation: 10 minutes

Cooking: 10 minutes

Servings: 4

Ingredients:

- 4 boneless, skinless chicken breasts.
- 2 C. All-purpose flour.
- 2 tsp. Salt.
- 2 tsp. Black pepper.
- 1 C. Buttermilk.
- ½ C. Water.
- 3 to 4 inches of oil for frying

Instructions:

1. Heat the oil to 350 degrees Fahrenheit in a big saucepan or a deep fryer.
2. Combine the salt, flour and pepper in a mixing dish to make seasoned flour.
3. In another basin, combine the buttermilk and water.
4. If your chicken breasts aren't the same size, place them between two sheets of wax paper and use a meat pounder to gently pound them out until they are. Cooking times will be more consistent as a result of this.
5. Using a paper towel, pat dry the chicken breasts.
6. Dredge the chicken in the seasoned flour after seasoning it with salt and pepper.
7. Buttermilk the floured chicken.
8. Dredge the chicken in the seasoned flour once more.
9. Deep-fry the chicken pieces in the hot oil for 7 to 8 minutes, or until done. While cooking the chicken breasts, flip them over to ensure that both sides are golden brown.
10. When it's done, remove the chicken from the oil and drain it on a wire rack.

Nutrition: Calories: 500. Total Fat: 30 g. Carbs: 50 g. Protein: 9 g. Fiber: 1 g. Sodium: 1240.

3. Creamy Chicken and Rice Casserole

Preparation: 10 minutes

Cooking: 45 minutes

Servings: 4

Ingredients:

- 2 C. cooked rice.
- 1 Onion (diced)
- 1 can cream of mushroom soup.
- 1 jar chicken gravy.
- 1 1/2 lb. chicken breasts (cut into strips).

Instructions:

1. Preheat the oven to 350°F.
2. Cook the rice.
3. Whether it's just about complete, throw in the diced onion.
4. Spray baking dishes with non-stick cooking spray.
5. Cover the bottom of the baking dish with your rice and place the cut-up chicken on top.
6. Spread the undiluted cream of mushroom soup over the chicken.
7. In a bowl, mix together the chicken gravy using 1 C. warm water, making sure to get all the lumps out. Pour it on top of the casserole.
8. Cover with foil and then bake in the oven for 45 min. at 350°F or until the chicken is totally cooked.

Nutrition: Calories: 111. Total Fat: 23 g. Carbs: 12 g. Protein: 81 g. Fiber: 0 g.

4. Chicken and Dumplings

Preparation: 35 minutes

Cooking: 5 minutes

Servings: 6

Ingredients:

- 6 C. chicken broth
- 2 ribs of celery (broken in half)
- 1 lb. boneless skinless chicken breasts (cut in half)
- 1 Tbsp. baking powder
- 1/2 medium onion (chopped)
- 3 C. flour
- 1 C. + 2 Tbsp milk
- 1 1/4 tsp. salt
- Salt and pepper to taste

Instructions:

1. Combine broth, celery, onion, and chicken breasts in a stockpot or Dutch oven.
2. Bring to a boil, then reduce to a low heat and cook for about 15 min, partially covered, until the chicken breasts are cooked thoroughly. Prepare the dumplings while the chicken is cooking. Combine baking powder, flour and salt in a medium mixing bowl. Add the milk and stir until it forms a shaggy dough.
3. Roll the dough out onto a floured board to a thickness of about 1/4 inch.
4. Using a pizza cutter, cut the dough into 1 to 2 inch wide strips or squares.
5. Transfer the chicken to a chopping board after it has finished cooking. Remove and discard the onion chunks and celery pieces.
6. Add the dough strips to the simmering liquid and cook, stirring occasionally, for about 20–30 mins, or until the dumplings are cooked through and the broth has thickened to a gravy-like consistency.
7. Shred or chop the chicken and return it to the saucepan while the dumplings are boiling.
8. Season with salt and pepper to taste, then serve immediately.

Nutrition: Calories: 425. Total Fat: 9 g. Carbs: 50 g. Protein: 36 g. Fiber: 3 g. Sodium 1780

5. Chicken Pot Pie

 Preparation: 5 minutes

 Cooking: 25 minutes

 Servings: 6

Ingredients:

- 2 Tbsp. canola oil.
- 1 onion (chopped).
- 1 sheet refrigerated pie crust
- 1/2 C. flour.
- 1 tsp. poultry seasoning.

- 1 can (14 ½ oz.) chicken broth
- 3/4 C. 2% milk.
- 3 C. cooked chicken (cubed).
- 2 C. Frozen mixed vegetables.

Instructions:

1. Preheat the oven to 450 °F. Heat the oil in a large saucepan over medium-high heat. Cook and stir in the onion until it becomes soft.

2. Mix in the flour and poultry seasoning until it's all mixed in. Then, slowly whisk in the broth and milk.

3. Bring to a boil, stirring regularly; cook and stir for 2-3 minutes, or until the mix has thickened. Place the chicken and vegetables in the pot.

4. Transfer to a greased 9-inch deep-dish pie plate and top with crust. Edges should be trimmed, sealed, and fluted. Make slits in the crust.

5. Bake for 15-20 mins, or until the crust is golden brown and the filling has risen to the top.

Nutrition: Calories: 442. Total Fat: 22 g. Carbs: 39 g. Protein: 28 g. Sodium: 528 mg.

6. Green Chili Jack Chicken

 Preparation: 10 minutes

 Cooking: 20 minutes

 Servings: 2

. . . .

Ingredients:

- 1 lb. Chicken strips.
- 1 tsp. Chili powder.
- 4 oz. green chilies.
- 2 C. Monterey Jack cheese.
- ¼ C. salsa.

. . . .

Instructions:

1. Spray a medium-sized skillet with cooking spray.
2. Sprinkle the chicken with all the chili powder and cook until they have lost their pink color.
3. Reduce the heat, then place the green chilies in and cook until heated through.
4. Add the cheese over the chiles and cook until the cheese is melted.
5. Put on a dish and serve with salsa on the side.

. . . .

Nutrition: Calories: 516. Total Fat: 23 g. Carbs: 8 g. Protein: 64 g. Sodium: 698 mg.

7. Broccoli Cheddar Chicken

 Preparation: 10 minutes

 Cooking: 45 minutes

 Servings: 4

Ingredients:

- 4 boneless skinless chicken breasts.

- ½ tsp. seasoned salt.

- 4 Tbsp. melted butter

- 1 ½ C. milk.

- 10.25 cans cheddar cheese soup.

- 4 oz. cheddar cheese (shredded)

- 8 oz. Frozen broccoli (chopped and defrosted).

- 1 ½ C. crushed Ritz crackers, (crushed).

Instructions:

1. Preheat the oven to 350 °F.

2. Follow the directions on the can of Cheddar cheese soup mix (one can of soup mix to one can of milk). In a 9 by 13-inch baking dish, place the chicken breasts. Season the chicken with a pinch of salt and pepper. 3/4 of the prepared soup should be poured over the chicken breasts.

3. Toss broccoli into the chicken once it has been covered in cheddar soup. Butter the Ritz crackers (with melted butter) and sprinkle them over the broccoli. Before baking, add the remaining soup mix. Bake for 45 minutes, or until the chicken is done. (Check the chicken by cutting the thickest part and inspecting it for color consistency.) Sprinkle shredded cheddar cheese on top of the chicken after it has been taken from the oven.

Nutrition: Calories: 1340. Total Fat: 69 g. Carbs: 93 g. Protein: 90 g.

8. Grilled Catfish

Preparation: 20 minutes

Cooking: 10 minutes

Servings: 4

Ingredients:

- 1 lb. catfish fillets
- ¼ C. lemon juice
- 2 Tbsp. chili powder
- 1 C. white wine
- 2 tsp. ground black pepper
- 2 Tbsp. dry mustard
- ½ C. cilantro (chopped)
- ½ tsp. salt
- 2 Tbsp. olive oil

Instructions:

1. Preheat the grill or the oven broiler.
2. Except for the catfish, combine the remaining ingredients in a medium mixing bowl.
3. Pour the marinade over the fish fillets and let aside for at least 15 minutes to marinate.
4. Arrange the catfish fillets on a slotted tray in a tidy manner. This will allow the fillets to drain.
5. Grill the fillets for 3 minutes on each side, or until fully done. Before cooking, make sure the grill is adequately greased.
6. While grilling, baste with the reserved marinade.
7. Serve with veggies of your choice.

Nutrition: Calories: 300. Total Fat: 17 g. Carbs: 9 g. Protein: 24 g. Sodium: 431 mg.

9. Lemon Pepper Trout

Preparation: 10 minutes

Cooking: 20 minutes

Servings: 4

Ingredients:

- 4 (6 oz.) fillets rainbow trout
- 4 C. flour
- 2 Tbsp. lemon pepper
- ½ tsp. dried thyme
- ½ tsp. cayenne pepper
- 1 lemon

- 1 tsp. onion powder
- ¼ C. grated lemon zest (divided)
- 1 ½ Tbsp. salt
- ½ C. lemon juice
- ½ C. extra-virgin olive oil

Instructions:

1. Combine thyme, lemon pepper, flour, salt, cayenne, and half of the lemon zest in a large mixing bowl. In a small dish, combine the lemon juice and remaining lemon zest and soak the fish fillets for about 1 minute.

2. In a large skillet, heat the oil over medium heat. Both sides of the trout fillets should be coated in the flour mixture. Remove any excess and lay the fillets in the heated oil. Cook for 3 to 4 minutes on each side, or until golden brown and flaky with a fork. Remove the lemon juice that hasn't been used.

3. Before serving, remove from the skillet and drain on paper towels for a few minutes. Serve with a wedge of lemon on top of each serving.

Nutrition: Calories: 980. Total Fat: 39 g. Protein: 49 g. Carbs 104. Sodium: 3400 mg.

10. Roast Beef Sandwiches with Mashed Potatoes

 Preparation: 7 minutes

 Cooking: 3 minutes

 Servings: 4

Ingredients:

- 1-pound sliced deli roast beef.
- 4 slices Italian bread (1/2 inches thick).
- 1 package (3 ¾ oz) creamy butter, instant mashed potatoes.
- 2 cans beef gravy.
- 1 can mushroom stems and pieces (drained)

Instructions:

1. Combine the mushrooms, gravy, and meat in a 2-quart mixing bowl.
2. Microwave on high (covered) for 2-3 minutes, or until well heated.
3. In the meantime, cook the potatoes according to the package directions.
4. Distribute the bread among the four plates.
5. Spread the beef mixture on top of the bread.
6. Serve with a side of potatoes.

Nutrition: Calories: 350. Fat: 8 g. Cholesterol: 79 mg. Sodium: 2045 mg. Carbohydrate: 40 g. Protein: 32 g.

11. Tomato, Cucumber and Onion Salad

 Preparation: 10 minutes

 Cooking: 0 minutes

 Servings: 3

Ingredients:

- 16 ounces of grape tomatoes.
- 3 cucumbers sliced (1/4 inch)
- 1/2 C. White onion, chopped finely.
- 1 C. White vinegar.
- 2 tbsp. Italian dressing.
- 1/2 C. sugar.

Instructions:

1. Whisk together the sugar, vinegar, and Italian dressing in a small bowl.
2. Add the sliced cucumbers, tomatoes, and onions.
3. Allow vegetables to marinate for about 1 hour before serving.

Nutrition: Calories: 123. Total Fat: 1 g. Carbs: 27 g. Protein: 1 g. Sodium: 58 mg.

12. Macaroni and Cheese

 Preparation: 25 minutes

 Cooking: 2 hours

 Servings: 16

Ingredients:

- 3 C. elbow macaroni (uncooked)
- 1 package (16 oz) Velveeta (cubed)
- 2 C. shredded Mexican cheese blend
- 2 C. shredded cheddar cheese
- 1 ¾ C. whole milk
- 1 can (12 oz.) evaporated milk
- ¾ C. melted butter
- 3 large eggs (lightly beaten)

Instructions:

1. According to package directions, cook macaroni for al dente; drain.
2. Transfer to a greased 5-qt. slow cooker. Stir in the remaining ingredients.
3. Cook, covered, on low 2 to 2 ½ hours or until a thermometer reads at least 160°F, stirring once

Nutrition: Calories: 390. Protein: 19 g. Carbs: 18 g. Fat: 26 g. Sodium: 660 mg.

13. Brussels Sprout N' Kale Salad

Preparation: 10 minutes

Cooking: 5 minutes

Servings: 8

Ingredients:

- 5 C. kale (finely sliced)
- 1 lb. Brussels sprouts.
- ½ C. craisins.
- ¾ C. Pecans.

Maple vinaigrette:

- 1/2 C. Olive oil.
- 3/4 C. vinegar (white)
- ½ C. Maple syrup.
- 1 ½ tsp. Dijon mustard.

Instructions:

1. Kale should be washed and dried with a towel.
2. Remove the stem from each kale stalk and discard it. The stems might be brittle and woody.
3. Roll the leaves like a cigar and slice them as finely as possible, then break up the lengthy pieces with a couple of horizontal slashes.
4. Sprouts should be washed and dried. Remove the stem end. Brussel sprouts should be split in half with the stem end down. Place the flattened sprout on the cutting board and slice as thinly as possible.
5. Toss sliced kale and Brussel sprouts with Craisins and nuts in a large mixing bowl.
6. Combine maple syrup, white vinegar, sugar, vegetable oil, salt, and dijon mustard in a small bowl. Whisk until everything is fully combined.
7. Pour the well-blended dressing over the veggies and toss to combine. Before serving, cover and chill for at least 30 minutes.

Nutrition: Calories: 350. Protein: 6 g. Carbs: 46 g. Fat: 22g.

14. Green Beans

Preparation: 10 minutes

Cooking: 50 minutes

Servings: 8

Ingredients:

- 1/4 lb. sliced bacon.
- 3 (42 oz) cans of green beans.
- ¼ C. onion (chopped).
- 1/2 tsp. Fresh ground black pepper.
- 1 tsp. Sugar.
- 1/2 tsp. Salt.

Instructions:

1. Cook bacon in a 2-quart pot over medium heat until it is gently browned but not crunchy.
2. After the bacon has browned, stir in the green beans, salt, sugar, and pepper.
3. On top of the green beans, place the onion.
4. Bring to a light boil, covered with a lid.
5. Reduce the heat to low and cook the beans for 45 minutes. Cooking the green beans for 45 minutes on a very low simmer will blend the flavors.

Nutrition: Calories: 55. Protein: 2 g. Carbs: 12 g. Sodium: 161 mg.

15. Pinto Beans

 Preparation: 10 minutes

 Cooking: 5 hours

 Servings: 10

Ingredients:

- 2 C. bag dry pinto beans.
- 1 lb. ham hocks.
- 1 ½ tsp Salt.
- 1 tbs Sugar.
- 8 C. Water

Instructions:

1. Cook ham hocks and sugar in a pan with enough water to cover them. Cook for about 2 hours on low heat.

2. Pull the meat apart using two forks when it's tender to remove the meat from the fat, skin, and bones. Return the meat to the broth and place it in the freezer until bean day.

3. Dry pinto beans should be washed and sorted. Add the beans, 8 cups water, the salt, and the ham to the pot with the broth from above. Bring to a boil, then reduce to a low heat and cook for 3 hours, or until the vegetables are soft.

Nutrition: Calories: 258. Protein: 20 g. Carbs: 23 g. Fat: 10 g. Sodium: 360 mg.

16. Baby Carrots

 Preparation: 10 minutes

 Cooking: 45 minutes

 Servings: 8

Ingredients:

- 2 lb. fresh baby carrots.
- 1 Tbsp. Brown Sugar.
- 2 Tbsp. Margarine.
- 1 tsp. Salt.

Instructions:

1. Carrots should be rinsed and placed in a 2-quart saucepan. Pour just enough water to cover the carrots' tops. Cover the pan with a lid and bring to a boil over medium heat.

2. Reduce to a low heat and cook for 30 to 45 minutes, or until the carrots are soft when pierced with a fork. Pour off half of the water when the carrots are soft. Replace the cover on the pan and add the margarine, sugar, and salt.

3. Cook until the vegetables are thoroughly soft but not mushy. If necessary, season with more salt. Add a pinch of ground nutmeg for a special touch.

Nutrition: Calories: 75. Protein: 0 g. Carbs: 11 g. Fat: 4 g. Sodium: 420 mg.

17. Mashed Potatoes

Preparation: 10 minutes

Cooking: 10 minutes

Servings: 4

Ingredients:

- 2 1/2 pounds russet potatoes.
- 4 tbsp. Margarine butter.
- 1/4 C. Milk.
- 1 tsp. Salt.
- 1/2 tsp. Black pepper.

Instructions:

1. Wash and peel the potatoes. Slice the potatoes into 1-inch pieces and place them into a pot.
2. Fill the pot with water, add adequate water to cover the potatoes, and add another 1/2 inches of water.
3. Cook them on medium-high heat for about 7-10 min. Drain the potatoes.
4. Put potatoes into a bowl with the rest of the ingredients and press the potatoes with a potato masher.

Nutrition: Calories: 338. Protein: 7 g. Carbs: 55 g. Fat: 2 g. Sodium: 740 mg.

18. Baby Limas

 Preparation: 5 minutes

 Cooking: 30 minutes

 Servings: 8

Ingredients:

- 1 C. Water.
- 1 chicken bouillon cube.
- 2 slices bacon.
- 1 clove garlic.
- 1/2 tsp. red pepper flakes.
- 1/2 tsp. Onion powder.
- 1 tsp. Sugar.
- 1/2 tsp. Black pepper.
- 1 (16-ounce) bag of frozen baby lima beans.

Instructions:

1. Bring water and bouillon cubes to a boil in a big pot.
2. Add the remaining ingredients. Stir and cover. Reduce heat to maintain a simmer.
3. Cook for 30 min., stir and then add a little more water if needed.
4. Season to taste with salt. Discard the bacon and garlic cloves.

Nutrition: Calories: 290. Protein: 10 g. Carbs: 29 g. Fat: 15 g. Sodium: 320 mg.

19. Coleslaw

Preparation: 10 minutes

Cooking: 0 minutes

Servings: 8

Ingredients:

- 2 C. Shredded cabbage.
- 1/2 C. Shredded lettuce.
- 1/2 C. Shredded purple cabbage.
- 1 C. Miracle Whip.
- 1 tsp. Celery seeds.
- 1/2 tsp. Salt.
- 1/2 tsp. Pepper.
- 1/3 C. sugar.
- 1/4 C. Vinegar.
- 1/4 C. Buttermilk.
- 1/4 C. Milk.
- 4 tsp. Lemon juice.

Instructions:

1. Put the cabbages, lettuce and purple cabbage in a large mixing bowl.
2. Stir in the Miracle Whip, celery seeds, salt, sugar, pepper, vinegar, buttermilk, milk, and lemon juice.
3. Toss back to fully blend.
4. Refrigerate for about 3 h. prior to serving.

Nutrition: Calories: 85. Protein: 1 g. Carbs: 15 g. Fat: 1 g.

20. Cheese 'n' Grits Casserole

 Preparation: 10 minutes

 Cooking: 30 minutes

 Servings: 8

. . . .

Ingredients:

- 4 C. Water.
- 1 C. Uncooked old-fashioned grits.
- 1/2 tsp. Salt.
- 1/2 C. 2% milk.
- 1/4 C. butter, melted.
- 2 large eggs, lightly beaten.
- 1 C. shredded cheddar cheese.
- 1 tbsp. Worcestershire sauce.
- 1/8 tsp. Cayenne pepper.
- 1/8 tsp. Paprika.

. . . .

Instructions:

1. Preheat the oven to 350°F.
2. In a big saucepan, bring water to a boil. Gradually stir in the grits and salt.
3. Low heat; cover and cook until thickened, 5-7 min. Cool slightly. Gradually whisk in milk, butter, and eggs. Stir in the cheese, Worcestershire sauce and cayenne.
4. Transfer to a greased 2-qt. baking dish. Sprinkle with paprika.
5. Bake, uncovered, until bubbly, 30-35 minutes.
6. Let stand 10 min. before serving.

. . . .

Nutrition: Calories: 205. Protein: 6 g. Carbs: 15 g. Fat: 10 g.

21. Loaded Potato Salad

 Preparation: 10 minutes

 Cooking: 35 minutes

 Servings: 8

Ingredients:

- 2 lb. russet potatoes
- 2 stalks celery (thinly sliced)
- ¼ C. pickle chopped or pickle relish
- 2 hard-boiled eggs (plus one for garnish, if desired)
- 1 tsp. salt
- 1 C. mayonnaise
- ¼ C. onions (chopped)

Instructions:

1. Remove any dirt from the potatoes by washing them. In a large saucepan, boil potatoes. Fill the pot with enough water to cover the potatoes by an inch.

2. Cook potatoes for 30 minutes on medium-high heat. After 30 minutes, pierce the potatoes with a fork to see whether they are done. They're done when a fork easily passes through them. If the fork doesn't easily pass through, cook for another five minutes and test again. When the potatoes are done, set them aside to cool until they are easily handled. Remove the skin by rubbing it.

3. Place the potatoes in a bowl, diced. Add the sliced egg, celery, onions, and chopped pickles/relish to the bowl. Mix in 1 teaspoon of salt and 1 cup of mayonnaise, and mix well. thoroughly. If preferred, top with more sliced egg and a sprinkling of paprika.

Nutrition: Calories: 300. Fat: 24 g. Carbs: 23 g. Protein: 5 g. Sodium: 540 mg.

Chapter 3: Dinner Recipes

1. Beef Stew

 Preparation: 20 minutes

 Cooking: 90 minutes

 Servings: 6

Ingredients:

- 1 lb. stewed beef in medium-sized pieces.
- 3 tbsp. Vegetable oil (divided).
- Salt and pepper to taste.
- 1/2 C. Flour.
- 1 onion (sliced).
- 4 medium potatoes (cut into pieces).
- 5 carrots (peeled and cut into pieces).
- 2 large turnips (cut into pieces).
- 1 quart of beef stock.
- 1 beef bouillon cube.
- 1/4 tsp. dried thyme.
- 1/4 C. Ketchup.
- 1 C. Peas.

Instructions:

1. Mix the flour with pepper and salt to taste and toss together with the meat.
2. Add 2 tbsp. oil into a huge pot, and over moderate-high heat, brown beef in flour, add all of the flour.
3. Stir frequently, so the meat and flour don't burn off, but brown well. Move meat to a plate.
4. Insert the final tablespoon of oil and sauté the onion until translucent, scraping with a spoonful up and browning bits from the meat.
5. Move the meat back to the pot, add the carrots, potatoes, and turnips.
6. Add the stock, thyme, and ketchup. Stir well to blend.
7. Simmer over low heat, frequently stirring for 1 1/2 hours. Correct seasoning.
8. Insert frozen peas prior to serving. Stir to defrost and serve.

Nutrition: Calories: 534. Carbohydrates: 61 g. Protein: 43 g. Fat: 18 g. Sodium: 1029 mg.

2. Meat Loaf

 Preparation: 15 minutes

 Cooking: 60-90 minutes

 Servings: 8

Ingredients:

- 2 lb. lean ground beef.
- 1/2 C. Finely chopped bell pepper (optional)
- 1/2 C. onion(chopped).
- 1 tsp. Salt.
- 1 C. of crushed Ritz crackers (48 crackers total).
- 1 C. torn sharp cheddar cheese (shredded).

- 1/4 tsp. Black pepper.
- 2 eggs.
- 1/2 C. Milk.
- 1/2 Tbsp. olive oil

for the topping:

- 1/2-3/4 C. Ketchup.
- 1 tsp. Mustard
- 2 Tbsp. Brown sugar.

Instructions:

1. Preheat oven 350 degrees F.
2. In a small pan, sauté for about 5 minutes, the diced peppers and onions with the olive oil until softened. They have a more subtle flavor and texture as a result of this. Remove from the oven and set aside to cool.
3. In a large mixing bowl, whisk together the crushed crackers, bell peppers, whisked eggs, onions, milk, cheese, and salt/pepper.
4. Mix in the ground beef until it is completely mixed. We want tender results, so don't overwork the meat.
5. Before place it in a loaf pan, shape it into a loaf. If you don't use a loaf pan, the bread may break apart. It also takes much longer to cook, resulting in it becoming dry. Bake for 30

minutes. While it's baking, mix together the topping ingredients and set them aside.

6. Remove the meatloaf from the pan and brush the topping on. Add another 30-40 minutes to the baking time. (When it hits 155 °F, remove it.)

7. Allow it to rest in the loaf pan for 15 minutes before slicing. During this time, the temperature will rise by 8-10°F. When you slice in too early, the juices run out as well. Before you slice it, make sure it's 160°F in the middle.

8. Enjoy with a side of creamy mashed potatoes!

. . . .

Nutrition: Calories: 450. Carbohydrates: 17 g. Protein: 27 g. Fat: 33 g. Cholesterol: 121 mg.

3. Roast Beef

 Preparation: 15 minutes

 Cooking: 8-10 hours

 Servings: 4-6

Ingredients:

- 3 lb. Chuck Roast.
- 1/2 Can Beef Broth.
- 1 C. Flour.
- 2 tbsp. Olive Oil.
- 1 or 2 cloves garlic.
- 1 onion, chopped.
- 1 Bay Leaf.
- 1/2 tsp. Garlic Powder.
- Salt and Pepper.

Instructions:

1. Wash chuck roast.
2. Season with pepper, garlic powder and salt.
3. Cover with flour and put it into an oiled skillet and brown lightly on both sides.
4. Add diced onions to the skillet.
5. Transfer everything to a greased crock-pot and stir in whole garlic cloves and bay leaf.
6. Pour in 1/2 cans of beef broth over the roast and season with salt and pepper.
7. Cover and cook on low for 8 to 10 h.

Nutrition: Calories: 480. Fat: 29 g. Carbohydrate: 10 g. Protein: 45 g.

4. Grilled Pork Chops

 Preparation: 20 minutes

 Cooking: 10 minutes

 Servings: 4

Ingredients:

- 1/4 C. Kosher salt.
- 1/4 C. Sugar.
- 2 C. Water.
- 2 C. Ice water.
- 4 center-cut pork rib chops (1 inch thick and 8 oz each).
- 2 tsp. Canola oil.

Basic rub:

- 3 tbsp. Paprika.
- 1 tsp. Each garlic powder, onion powder, ground cumin, and ground mustard.
- 1 tsp. Ground pepper.
- 1/2 tsp. Ground chipotle pepper

Instructions:

1. In a large saucepan, mix sugar, salt, and 2 C. water, cook, and stir over moderate heat until the sugar and salt have melted. Remove from heat.
2. Insert 2 C. ice water to cool brine to room temperature.
3. Put pork chops in a big resealable plastic bag; insert cooled brine.
4. Seal bags, pushing out as much air as you can; turn to coat chops.
5. Set at a 13x9-in. Baking dish. Refrigerate 8-12 hours.
6. Remove the chops from the brine, wash and pat dry. Discard brine.
7. Sweep both sides of the chops with oil. In a small bowl, combine the rubbing ingredients; rub over the pork chops. Let stand at room temperature for about 30 min.
8. Grill the chops in an oiled rack, covered, over moderate heat, for 4-6 mins. on each side or until a thermometer read 145°F. Let's stand 5 min before working out.

Nutrition: Calories: 306. Fat: 20 g. Cholesterol: 74 mg. Sodium: 136 mg. Carb: 6 g. Protein: 33 g.

5. Mushroom Braised Pot Roast

 Preparation: 10 minutes

 Cooking: 90 minutes

 Servings: 10

Ingredients:

- 4 lb. chuck roast.
- 2 Tbsp. Butter.
- 2 Tbsp. Vegetable oil.
- 1/4 tsp. Pepper.
- 1 C. onion(sliced).

- 2 C. Beef broth.
- 2 Tbsp. Gravy master.
- 1/2 tsp. Salt.
- 1 lb. cremini mushrooms (chopped)
- 1/2 tsp. Salt.

Instructions:

1. Season the roast with salt and pepper. Fill a large Dutch oven halfway with vegetable oil.
2. Sear the roast on all sides until it is golden brown. Add 1 chopped onion, 2 cups beef broth, and 2 tablespoons Gravy Master to the Dutch oven.
3. Preheat the oven to 350 degrees Fahrenheit.
4. For every pound of meat, cook the roast for 30 minutes.
5. When you remove the roast from the oven saute 1 pound of sliced mushrooms butter. While the mushrooms are sauteing, season them with 1/2 teaspoon of salt.
6. Add the mushrooms to the roast when they're done.

Nutrition: Calories: 398. Carbohydrates: 4 g. Protein: 40 g. Fat: 29 g. Cholesterol: 134 mg. Sodium: 790 mg

6. Shepherd's Pie

Preparation: 15 minutes

Cooking: 50 minutes

Servings: 4

Ingredients:

- 1 tsp. salt
- 1 1/2 lb. ground round beef
- 3 large (1 1/2 to 2 lb.) potatoes, peeled and quartered
- 1/2 C. beef broth
- 8 Tbsp. (1 stick) butter (divided)

- 1 medium onion (chopped)
- 1 to 2 C. mixed vegetables, such as diced carrots, corn, or peas
- 1 tsp. Worcestershire sauce
- Pepper and/or other seasonings

Instructions:

1. In a medium-sized pot, place the potatoes. Cover with a layer of cold water of at least an inch thick. Add a teaspoon of salt to the mixture. Bring to a boil, then reduce to a low heat and cook until the potatoes are cooked. It will take about 20 minutes. Preheat the oven to 400 degrees Fahrenheit.

2. Meanwhile, melt 4 tablespoons butter in a large sauté skillet over medium heat. Then add the onions and cook until tender (about 6 to 10 minutes).

3. Vegetables should be added according to their cooking time if you're using them. Carrots should be cooked alongside onions because they take the same amount of time to cook as onions.

4. Combine ground beef to the pan with the onions and vegetables. Cook until the meat is no longer pink. If necessary, drain any extra fat from the pan (only 1 tablespoon should remain). Salt & pepper to taste.

5. Combine the Worcestershire sauce and beef broth in a mixing bowl. Reduce the heat to low and bring the broth to a simmer. Cook for 10 minutes, uncovered, adding more beef broth as

needed to prevent the meat from drying out.

6. Taste the cooked filling and season with additional salt, pepper, Worcestershire sauce, or other ingredients as desired.

7. Remove the potatoes from the pot when they are done cooking. Then place them in a bowl with the remaining 4 Tbsp. of butter. Taste and season with salt and pepper after mashing with a fork or potato masher.

8. In a 9 x 13-inch casserole, spread the cooked mixture in an equal layer.

9. On top of the ground beef, spread the mashed potatoes. With a fork, rough up the surface of the mashed potatoes to create peaks that will brown nicely. You may also make creative designs in the mashed potatoes using a fork.

10. Place in the preheated oven for 30 minutes, or until browned and bubbling. Broil the mashed potatoes for the last few minutes if necessary to brown the surface.

. . . .

Nutrition: Calories: 870. Fat: 48 g. Protein: 56. Carbohydrates: 52 g

7. Grilled Chicken Tenderloins

 Preparation: 5 minutes

 Cooking: 10 minutes

 Servings: 6

Ingredients:

- 1 lb. chicken breast tenders.
- 2 C. Italian dressing.
- 2 Tbsp. fresh lime juice.
- 6 Tbsp. Honey.

Instructions:

1. Combine the lime juice, Italian dressing, and honey in a mixing bowl.
2. Place the chicken in a freezer bag. Refrigerate for a few hours to overnight after pouring the marinade over the chicken.
3. Get the grill ready. Remove the chicken from the marinade and toss it out.
4. Cook the chicken for 10 to 12 minutes, or until it reaches an internal temperature of 165°F.

Nutrition: Calories: 400. Fat: 21 g. Cholesterol: 141 mg. Sodium: 871 mg. Carbohydrate: 11 g. Protein: 49 g.

8. Veal Pot Roast

 Preparation: 1 hour

 Cooking: 2 hours

 Servings: 10

Ingredients:

- 4 Tbsp. Butter.
- 6 lb. veal rump roast.
- 2 C. onions (chopped).
- 2 C. Sour cream.
- 3 C. Chicken stock (divided).
- 2 Tbsp. dill weed.
- 1 tsp. Seasoned salt.
- 1/4 tsp. red pepper flakes.

Instructions:

1. Dissolve the butter and brown the roast, in a Dutch oven.
2. Then remove from the roast and saute the onion in the remaining butter until light brown.
3. Add in the sour cream, 2 cups chicken stock, and the seasonings.
4. Cook the roast with the sauce in the same pot.
5. Simmer, covered, for 2-3 hours, or until fork-tender.
6. As needed, add the remaining chicken stock.
7. Serve with the sauce on the side.

Nutrition: Calories: 673. Fat: 13 g. Cholesterol: 254 mg. Sodium: 516 mg. Carbohydrate: 7 g. Protein: 79 g.

9. Country Fried Steak (Chicken Fried Steak)

Preparation: 5 minutes

Cooking: 10 minutes

Servings: 4

Ingredients:

- 1 pound cube steak/minute steak.
- 1 C. Milk.
- 1 Tbsp. hot sauce.
- 3 C. Flour.
- 3 eggs

- 2 tsp. Baking powder.
- 2 tsp. Salt.
- 1 tsp. Pepper.
- 1/2 tsp. Cayenne pepper.
- Oil for frying.

Instructions:

1. Take two shallow bowls. In one, whisk the eggs, milk and hot sauce together. In the other, mix the flour, baking powder, salt, pepper and cayenne together.
2. Add the oil to a skillet that is about ¼ - ½ inches deep and heat on a medium-high heat.
3. Dredge the cube steak into flour and shake off the excess flour, coat into the egg mixture, and then coat into the flour mixture.
4. Place cube steak in hot oil. Let the steak fry for about 3-5 min. and lightly flip it, making sure the coating of the steak is entire.
5. Cook on different sides for 3-5 minutes.
6. Remove the steak and dry the oil in excess with paper. Cook the remaining steaks.
7. Serve with country gravy.

Nutrition: Calories: 600. Fat: 28 g. Cholesterol: 65 mg. Sodium: 1410 mg. Carbohydrates: 50 g. Protein: 37 g.

10. Breaded Fried Okra

 Preparation: 5 minutes

 Cooking: 10 minutes

 Servings: 6

Ingredients:

- 1 lb. okra.
- 1/3 C. Cornmeal.
- ½ Tbsp. garlic powder
- Salt and ground pepper (to taste)
- Oil for deep-fat frying.

Instructions:

1. Okra should be washed and sliced into quarter-inch slices.
2. Toss the okra with garlic powder and cornmeal. Season with salt and pepper to taste. Toss everything together.
3. Heat the oil in a medium saucepan over medium heat.
4. Fry the okra slices in the oil till golden brown.
5. To drain, place it in a slotted basket. Allow to cool for a few minutes before serving.
6. Enjoy with your favorite dipping sauce!

Nutrition: Calories: 140. Fat: 11 g. Sodium: 7 mg. Carbohydrate: 14 g. Protein: 3 g.

11. Apple Cider BBQ Chicken

Preparation: 10 minutes

Cooking: 30 minutes

Servings: 5

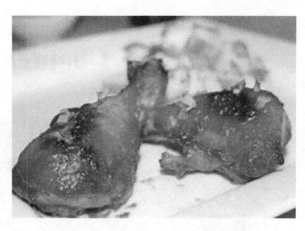

Ingredients:

- 36 oz. Chicken breasts, roughly.
- 1/3 c. Apple cider.
- 2/3 c. Barbecue sauce.
- 2 tbsp. Lemon juice.
- 2 tbsp. Apple cider vinegar.
- 2 tbsp. Dried rosemary.
- 2 tsp. Dried thyme.

- 1 tbsp. Garlic powder.
- 1 tsp. Dried basil.
- Salt and ground black pepper, to season.
- Cooking spray.

To Serve:

- 1 C. roasted carrots & and ¾ C. sautéed corn kernels.

Instructions:

1. Mix apple cider, apple cider vinegar, lemon juice, rosemary, thyme, garlic powder, barbeque sauce, and basil. Season with salt and pepper.
2. Add the chicken breasts, mix with the marinade and allow to overnight, sealed.
3. Preheat the grill and warrant that the chicken is at room temperature.
4. Grill first for about 3 -5 min. on each side.
5. Serve the chicken together with the roasted carrots and sautéed corn kernels.

Nutrition: Calories: 462. Fat: 22 g. Cholesterol: 136 mg. Sodium: 703 mg. Carbohydrate: 28 g, Protein: 47 g.

Chapter 4: Dessert Recipes

1. Campfire S'mores

Preparation: 15 minutes

Cooking: 40 minutes

Servings: 9

Ingredients:

Graham Cracker Crust:

- 2 C. graham cracker crumbs.
- 1/4 C. Sugar.
- 1/2 C. Butter.
- 1/2 tsp. Cinnamon.
- 1 small package of brownie mix (enough to get an 8×8-inch pan) or utilize the brownie ingredients listed below.

Brownie Mix:

- 1/2 C. Flour.
- 1/3 C. Cocoa.
- 1/4 tsp. Baking powder.
- 1/4 tsp. salt.
- 1/2 C. Butter.
- 1 C. Sugar.
- 1 tsp. Vanilla.
- 2 large eggs.

S'mores Topping:

- 9 marshmallows.
- 5 Hershey candy bars.

- 4 1/2 C. Vanilla ice cream.
- 1/2 C. Chocolate sauce.

Instructions:

1. Preheat your oven to 350°F.
2. In a mixing bowl, combine the Graham Cracker Crumbs, melted butter, cinnamon, and sugar.
3. Using parchment paper, line an 8-inch baking dish.
4. In the bottom of the pan, press the Graham Cracker Crumbs.
5. While you're making the brownies, put the pan in the oven.
6. To make the brownies, combine cocoa, baking powder, flour, and salt in a mixing bowl.
7. In a 10- to 12-cup saucepan, melt butter over medium heat. Stir in the sugar and vanilla extract, then add the eggs one by one. Combine the dry ingredients and nuts in a mixing bowl. Smoothly spread over the graham cracker crust.
8. In the preheated oven bake the brownies for 23 to 25 minutes. Allow the brownies to cool completely in the pan before serving.
9. When the brownies have totally cooled, gently remove them from the pan.
10. Make 9 equal servings out of the brownies. When you're ready to serve, top each brownie with a huge marshmallow and place it under the broiler in your oven.
11. Cook for a few minutes, or until the marshmallow starts to turn brown. Remove the marshmallow from the oven once it has browned, and top with 1/2 of a Hershey bar.
12. Serve with vanilla ice cream and a drizzle of chocolate sauce on top.

Nutrition: Calories: 890. Fat: 36 g. Carbs: 128 g. Protein: 9 g. Sodium: 670 mg.

2. Double Fudge Coca-Cola Cake

 Preparation: 25 minutes

 Cooking: 25 minutes

 Servings: 15

Ingredients:

- 2 C. all-purpose flour
- 2 C. sugar
- 1 tsp. baking soda
- 1/2 tsp. salt
- 1/2 tsp. ground cinnamon
- 1 can (12 oz.) cola
- 1 C. butter (cubed)
- 1/4 C. baking cocoa

- 2 large eggs
- 1/2 C. buttermilk
- 1 tsp. vanilla extract

  For glaze:

- 1 can (12 oz.) cola
- 1/2 C. butter (cubed)
- 1/4 C. baking cocoa
- 4 C. confectioners' sugar (sifted)

Instructions:

1. Preheat your oven to 350°F. Butter and flour a 9x13 cake pan. Set aside.

2. Into a big bowl, stir together sugar, flour, baking soda, salt and ground cinnamon.

3. Combine the cola, butter, and cocoa in a small saucepan and bring to a boil, stirring occasionally. Stir just until wet into the flour mixture.

4. In a small bowl, whisk together buttermilk, eggs, and vanilla extract until well combined; gradually add to the flour mixture, stirring constantly.

5. Transfer to prepared pan. Bake until a toothpick inserted in the center comes out clean, about 25-30 mins.

6. 15 minutes before the cake is done, make the glaze. Bring cola to a boil in a small saucepan; cook for 12-15 minutes, or until liquid is reduced to 1/2 C. After whisking in the butter and cocoa until the butter has melted, remove from the heat. Blend in the confectioners' sugar until it's completely smooth. Immediately pour over the hot cake.

Nutrition: Calories: 500. Fat: 22 g. Carbs: 80 g. Protein: 4 g. Sodium: 351 mg.

3. Banana Pudding

 Preparation: 10 minutes

 Cooking: 30 minutes

 Servings: 6

Ingredients:

- 3/4 C. sugar
- 1/3 C. all-purpose flour
- 3 C. whole milk
- 4 egg yolks (beaten)
- 3 Tbsp. butter
- 2 oz. cream cheese
- 2 tsp. vanilla extract

Banana Pudding:

- 2 large bananas
- 48 vanilla wafers

Whipped Cream:

- 1 tsp. sugar
- 1 C. heavy whipping cream whipped

Instructions:

Pudding:

1. Combine the sugar, flour, and milk in a heavy saucepan.
2. Cook, stirring constantly over medium heat, until the sauce has thickened and become bubbling.
3. Cook for another two minutes, stirring occasionally. Remove the pan from the heat.
4. In a small mixing bowl, whisk the egg yolks until pale and lighter in color.
5. 1 cup hot pudding mixture, will be slowly poured into the beaten eggs, whisking continually as the pudding is added.
6. Stir frequently as you slowly pour the egg yolk mixture into the pan with the rest of the pudding.

7. Cook, stirring regularly, until the mixture just begins to boil.

8. Combine the butter, cream cheese, and vanilla extract in a mixing bowl. Stir until all of the ingredients have been thoroughly combined.

9. Pour the pudding into a bowl and cover it with plastic wrap to keep it fresh.

10. Refrigerate the pudding until it reaches room temperature.

Whipped Cream:

1. In a mixing dish, combine 1 cup heavy whipping cream and 1 teaspoon sugar.

2. Whip the whipping cream with a whisk or a mixer until firm peaks form. If you aren't going to use it right away, keep it refrigerated.

Assembling the Banana Pudding:

1. Break vanilla wafers into 6 mason jars.

2. Cut bananas into slices and put four or five slices in each jar.

3. Top the bananas with a couple of teaspoons of pudding.

4. Repeat with the vanilla wafers, bananas, and pudding in each jar two more times.

5. Whipped cream is served on top.

6. If desired, garnish with banana slices, vanilla wafer crumbs, and/or vanilla wafer crumbs.

. . . .

Nutrition: Calories: 720. Fat: 2,8 g. Carbs: 86g. Protein: 12 g. Sodium: 351 mg.

4. Baked Apple Dumplings

Preparation: 25 minutes

Cooking: 40 minutes

Servings: 4

Ingredients:

- 1 (17 1/2 oz) package frozen puff pastry (thawed).
- 1 C. Sugar.
- 3/8 C. Dry breadcrumbs.
- 3 Tbsp. Ground cinnamon.
- 1 egg (beaten).
- 4 green apples (peeled, cored and halved).
- 1 C. Confectioners' sugar.
- 1 tsp. Vanilla extract.
- 1 pinch ground nutmeg.
- 3 tbsp. Milk.

Pecan Streusel:

- 2/3 C. Packed brown sugar.
- 2/3 C. All-purpose flour
- 5 tbsp. Melted butter.
- 2/3 C. toasted pecans (chopped)

Instructions:

1. Preheat oven to 425°F. Lightly grease a baking sheet.
2. Each pastry sheet should be 12x12 inches in size. To make 8 - 6 inch squares, cut the fabric into quarters.

3. Combine the bread crumbs, nutmeg, cinnamon, and sugar in a small mixing basin.

4. Brush a square of puff pastry with beaten egg.

5. 1 tablespoon of the bread crumb mixture should be placed in the center.

6. Place one apple half on top of the bread crumbs, core side down.

7. Add another tablespoon of the mixture on top.

8. Pull four corners of the pastry up and pinch the edges together to properly seal the seams. Rep with the rest of the apples.

9. Brush a beaten egg on each dumpling.

10. Serve with Pecan Streusel on top.

11. Bake for 15 minutes at 350°F, then decrease heat to 350°F and bake for another 25 minutes, or until gently browned.

12. Drizzle icing on top.

13. Allow to cool to room temperature before serving.

Pecan Streusel:

1. Combine the chopped toasted pecans, brown sugar, flour, and melted butter, in a small bowl. With a fork, combine the ingredients until they resemble moist crumbs. Follow the recipe's instructions. Make as much or as little as you want.

2. Combine confectioners' sugar, vanilla, and enough milk to produce a dripping consistency for the icing. Drizzle over the dumplings once they've cooled. Serve the same day.

Nutrition: Calories: 3200. Fat: 153 g. Carbs: 445 g. Protein: 34 g. Sodium: 1061 mg.

5. Ambrosia Fruit Salad

Preparation: 10 minutes

Cooking: 0 minutes

Servings: 1

Ingredients:

- 1/4 C. coconut
- 1/4 C. crushed pineapple
- 1 large orange sectioned or 2 to 3 mandarin oranges
- cherry to garnish if desired
- 2 tsp. powdered sugar to taste

Instructions:

1. In a small bowl mix pineapple and the orange sections. Sprinkle coconut over it. If desired garnish with cherry and serve.

Nutrition: Calories: 260. Fat: 7 g. Carbs: 52 g. Protein: 4 g. Sodium: 6 mg.

6. Biscuits

 Preparation: 15 minutes

 Cooking: 8-10 minutes

 Servings: 10

Ingredients:

- 2 1/4 C. pre-made biscuit/pancake mix
- 1 1/2 tsp. granulated sugar
- 2/3 C. buttermilk
- 2 Tbsp. unsalted butter (melted for brushing)
- 1 Tbsp. unsalted butter (melted)
- 4 Tbsp. flour (plus a bit extra for dusting and preventing stickiness

Instructions:

1. Spray a glass baking dish with nonstick spray and preheat the oven to 450 degrees. Combine the prepared biscuit/pancake mix, buttermilk, and sugar in a glass mixing bowl. Mix until everything is well blended.

2. Mix in the remaining 1 tablespoon of melted butter until thoroughly combined.

3. Sprinkle 1/4 cup all-purpose flour on a flat surface. Using the flour to coat the dough, knead it at least 20 times on the surface.

4. Roll the dough out to a thickness of 1/2 inch to 1 inch all over. Cut them into pieces with a circular biscuit cutter and arrange them on the plate.

5. Brush half of the 2 tablespoons of melted butter over the tops.

6. Bake for 8-10 minutes, or until light golden on top. Brush the tops with the remaining melted butter, after baking.

Nutrition (1 biscuit): Calories: 290. Fat: 15 g. Carbs: 37 g. Protein: 6 g. Sodium: 600 mg.

7. Chocolate Cherry Cobbler

Preparation: 10 minutes

Cooking: 45 minutes

Servings: 8

Ingredients:

- 21 oz. Cherry pie filling.
- 1 ½ C. Flour.
- 1/2 C. Sugar.
- 2 tsp. Baking powder.
- 1/2 tsp. Salt.
- 1/4 C. Cold butter.
- 1 egg (slightly beaten)
- 1/4 C. Milk.
- 6 oz. Semi-sweet chocolate morsels.
- ½ C. nuts (finely chopped)

Instructions:

1. Preheat your oven to 350° F.
2. Combine the flour, salt, butter, baking powder, and sugar in a large mixing bowl. Using a pastry blender, pulverize the crumbs until they are the size of small peas. Set aside.
3. Melt the chocolate chips and mix until dissolved using the microwave or stovetop.
4. Cool it down for around 5 minutes.
5. Mix chocolate with milk and egg until well blended.
6. Combine the two preparations (chocolate and flour) and mix.
7. In the bottom of a 2-quart casserole dish, spread the pie filling.
8. Over the cherries, drop chocolate batter in a haphazard pattern.
9. Add nuts to the top.
10. Preheat oven to 350°F and bake for 40–45 mins.

Nutrition: Calories: 468. Fat: 21 g. Carbs: 69 g. Protein: 9 g. Sodium: 231 mg.

8. Fried Apples

Preparation: 30 minutes

Cooking: 15 minutes

Servings: 10

Ingredients:

- 3 tbsp. Butter.
- 4 medium golden delicious apples.
- 1/4 C. Granulated sugar.
- 2 tbsp. Packed brown sugar.

- 1 tsp. Ground cinnamon.
- 1/4 tsp. Ground nutmeg.
- 1/2 C. Apple cider.
- 1 tbsp. Cornstarch.
- Also needed: 12-inch skillet.

Instructions:

1. Cut apples into 3/4-inch wedges (about 2 lb).
2. Melt a butter in a skillet over medium heat.
3. Toss in the apples, spices, and sugar. Mix and cover with a lid.
4. Cook for 11-14 minutes, occasionally stirring, until softened.
5. Put into a serving dish and cover to keep warm.
6. Beat the cider and cornstarch in a little cup; then add to the skillet, stirring continuously.
7. Simmer over medium heat for 30-60 seconds until it's thickened.
8. Pour the mixture over the apples before serving.

Nutrition: Calories: 113. Fat: 4 g. Carbs: 22 g. Protein: 0 g.

9. Pumpkin Custard N Ginger Snaps

Preparation: 30 minutes

Cooking: 35 minutes

Servings: 8

Ingredients:

- 8 egg yolks.
- 1/2 C. Granulated sugar.
- 1 C. Heavy whipping cream.
- 1 1/2 tsp. Pumpkin pie spice.
- 1/2 tsp. Pumpkin pie spice.
- 1 C. ginger snap cookies and about 8 ginger snap cookies that are whole.
- 1 Tbsp. Melted butter.
- 1 tsp. Vanilla.
- 1 3/4 C. Pure pumpkin puree - 1 (15 oz.) can of pure pumpkin.
- 1 tbsp. Granulated sugar.
- 1 3/4 C. Heavy whipping cream

Instructions:

1. Preheat your oven to 350°F.
2. In a glass bowl, whisk together the egg yolks until smooth.
3. Mix in 1 3/4 cup heavy cream, pumpkin, 1/2 cup sugar, pumpkin pie spice, and vanilla until thoroughly combined.
4. In a double boiler, cook the custard mixture, stirring constantly, until it has thickened and the spoon remains coated when pushed into the custard. Fill 8 custard plates or an 8 × 8 baking dish with the custard. Bake the custard for 20-25 minutes in custard dishes or 30-35 minutes in a regular oven (for baking dish).
5. Mix in the cup of ginger snaps and 1 tbsp. melted butter halfway through the baking process, then sprinkle the crumb mixture over the custard. Allow time for the custard to cool to room temperature before serving.
6. Whisked together 1 tablespoon granulated sugar, 1 cup whipping cream, and 1/4 teaspoon

pumpkin pie spice, just before serving, until the whipped cream is thickened.

7. Serve the pumpkin custard with pumpkin spice whipped cream.

. . . .

Nutrition: Calories: 490. Fat: 41 g. Carbs: 34 g. Protein: 7 g. Sodium: 116 mg.

10. Chocolate Pecan Pie

 Preparation: 10 minutes

 Cooking: 50 minutes

 Servings: 8

Ingredients:

- 3 eggs.
- 1/2 C. Sugar.
- 1 C. corn syrup (light).
- 3 Tbsp. Semi-sweet chocolate chips.
- 1 tsp. Vanilla extract.
- 1/4 C. Melted butter.
- 1 unbaked pie shell.
- 1 C. Pecans.
- 1/2 tsp. Salt.

Instructions:

1. Preheat your oven to 350°F.
2. In a medium-sized bowl, whisk together the eggs, then add the sugar and mix well.
3. Mix in salt, butter, vanilla, and corn syrup.
4. Fill the pie shell with pecans and chocolate chips.
5. Pour the pecan pie filling into the pie shell slowly.
6. When baked, the pecans will rise to the top.
7. Preheat oven to 350°F and bake for 50–60 mins.

Nutrition: Calories: 463. Fat: 9 g. Carbs: 66 g. Protein: 5 g. Sodium: 341 mg.

11. Strawberry Shortcake

 Preparation: 15 minutes

 Cooking: 0 minutes

 Servings: 4

Ingredients:

- 1 pre-made pound cake.
- 1 pint frozen sweetened strawberries.
- 4 scoops premium vanilla ice cream.
- 1 can whipped cream.

Instructions:

1. Strawberry shortcake is made by cutting two slices of pound cake in half and then slicing them in half.
2. In a bowl, arrange the four pieces of pound cake across from each other.
3. On top of the cake, place defrosted strawberries, one scoop of vanilla ice cream, and whipped cream.

Nutrition: Calories: 546. Fat: 19 g. Carbs: 81 g. Protein: 10 g. Sodium: 471 mg.

12. Peach Cobbler

Preparation: 10 minutes

Cooking: 60 minutes

Servings: 6-9

. . . .

Ingredients:

Batter:

- 1 C. Cracker Barrel Pancake mix.
- 1/2 tsp. Cinnamon.
- 1 C. Milk.
- 1/4 tsp. Nutmeg.
- 1/2 C. Melted butter.
- Filling:
- 2 cans (15 oz.) peach slices in heavy

syrup

- 1/4 C. sugar

Topping:

- 1/8 C. flour
- 1/2 C. brown sugar
- 1 Tbsp. softened butter
- 1/2 tsp. cinnamon
- sliced almonds

. . . .

Instructions:

1. Mix all batter ingredients in a bowl and whisk until well incorporated and light. Pour into a non-oiled 8 x 8 baking pan.

2. Drain peaches of syrup except for about 1 Tbsp. juice in each can. Then combine with sugar until it has melted. Pour over the batter but do not mix, batter will rise over peaches and juices on its own.

3. Mix all the topping components with your hands, lightly breaking up the almonds as you incorporate. Do not put on cobbler yet, as the almonds will burn!

4. Bake in the oven at 375°F for 45 mins. Then place the crumbles topping over the cobbler and bake for another 10-15 minutes. Take care not to burn the nuts.

5. Do not cool too much and serve by adding cinnamon ice cream. Enjoy!

. . . .

Nutrition: Calories: 481. Fat: 21 g. Carbs: 77 g Protein: 5 g. Sodium: 461 mg.

13. Carrot Cake

Preparation: 20 minutes

Cooking: 50 minutes

Servings: 24

Ingredients:

Cake:

- 2 C. carrots (finely shredded).
- 1 can (8 oz.) crushed pineapple with juice.
- ¾ C. Walnuts (chopped).
- 2 tsp. Baking powder.
- 1 1/4 C. Vegetable oil.
- 1 1/2 C. Sugar.
- 1/2 C. Brown sugar.
- 3 eggs.
- 3 C. Flour.
- 1/2 C. Coconut (finely shredded).
- 2 tsp. Baking soda.

- 2 tsp. Vanilla extract.
- 2 tsp. Ground cinnamon.
- 1/2 C. raisins (soaked in water until plump and drained).
- 1 tsp. Ground nutmeg.
- 1/2 tsp. Ground cloves.
- 1/2 tsp. Salt.

Cream Cheese Frosting:

- 8 oz. of cream cheese.
- 8 oz. Butter (softened).
- 1 tsp. Vanilla extract.
- 2 C. powdered sugar.
- 1/2 C. pecans for garnish (chopped).

Instructions:

1. Mix together baking powder, flour, nutmeg, salt, baking soda, cloves and cinnamon. In a big bowl, mix sugar, vanilla, oil, and eggs until creamy and fluffy.

2. Add walnuts, coconut, pineapple, carrots, and raisins and mix well. Regularly add the dry mixture half at a time until mixed through. Pour the batter into an oiled and floured 9"x13" pan and bake at 350°F for about 40 - 50 min.

3. For Cream Cheese Frosting: mix cream cheese and butter until creamy and fluffy. Add the vanilla and a few powdered sugars at a time until the frosting is light and fluffy. Let the cake cool, spread the frosting, and add the pecans.

Nutrition: Calories: 341. Fat: 16 g. Carbs: 51 g. Protein: 4 g. Sodium: 231 mg.

Conclusion

If you're a food-driven soul, then using an excellent meal is just one of the excellent joys of existence. This type of reward might even be regardless of the labor of dining outside; creating a booking, getting prepared, and, clearly, settling to purchase. However, the strangest time of all is when the Gourmet meals arrive, gliding through a busy dining area and preparing to be appreciated before being placed on the desk.

With attractively designed salads and exceptionally crispy, flavorful fried foods to elegant dinner and perfectly cooked legumes—great food for those restaurants always appears to have a bit extra to make it appear. But if you've ever had ill-ready food of the kind yourself, there's hope! With only a couple of straightforward tricks and suggestions, you might even cook superior cuisine in the kitchen. These are suggestions that might not look so powerful on their own but can change the way you prepare and create meals when they're used together.

These suggestions allow you to cook in the home just like an expert. Spending time with friends and family is very important to your own good whatsoever. It may avert loneliness related to depression, cardiovascular disease, and harmful illnesses. With just a small effort, cooking will be able to help you become much more sociable. Have your kids visit the kitchen along with you to provide them with easy tasks when they're young. And remember that the societal advantages which you get if your meal is prepared. A lot of men and women are pleased to have the ability to give homemade food to family and friends on different occasions.

Food is generally satisfied with a smiling face and a desire to go back. As you enhance your abilities and feel more confident as you cook, you may discover your culinary interests stretch past the kitchen. You're able to build a closer connection with your spouse since you're more involved with food preparation and might be encouraged to tell other people to split the dishes you've prepared. In any case, cooking could be a relaxing activity that you can love yourself.

Folks find personal satisfaction in cooking for themselves or view the encounter as a means to interact with their imagination. Cooking is not a dull thing, but a thing which gives them great joy. Cooking is interesting; it's a fire to share with friends and family with people you love. Cooking is really a gesture to be guarded, which, sadly, now risks being put aside for the hectic lifestyle we all lead and, consequently, for your demands about the brief moment.

Now, to get a healthy and nice family meal, we favor "fast food," prepared meals, or even a small "packed lunch". All this, maybe not a mistake, is a requirement now. Hopefully, these recipes have given you a couple of tips on the best way to recreate your favorite restaurant dishes at home. The publication is supposed to offer you a bit of inspiration and motivation to cook those foods from the conveniences of your home. You don't have to flake out to meet your cravings for all these foods that are popular. This way, you can know just where your meals went before arriving on the plate and will save yourself a couple of bucks in the procedure. And the next time you opt to dine out, you are going to dine in rather. By cooking in the home, you have to save effort and money, you have to control parts, and you also get to personalize every single meal. Bear in mind, the recipes in this publication are far more of a manual. Finally, you have to select how the following meal will taste and how to prepare it again.

Made in the USA
Las Vegas, NV
19 October 2023

79289264R00046